THE PLANES THE AXIS FLEW
IN WORLD WAR II

The Planes the Axis Flew
in World War II

DAVID C. COOKE

Dodd, Mead & Company · New York

PICTURE CREDITS

British Information Service, p. 11
Dornier-Werke, p. 10 (left)
Giorgio Apostolo, p. 8, 9, 21, 24, 25, 34, 35 (bottom), 48, 49 (bottom)
Imperial War Museum, p. 16, 17, 28, 38 (bottom), 39
Messerschmitt A. G., p. 52 (top and middle)
U.S. Air Force, p. 10 (right), 13 (bottom), 14, 15, 18, 19, 22 (top), 23, 26, 27, 29, 32, 33, 36, 37, 40, 41, 42, 43, 45, 52 (bottom), 53, 54, 57, 58, 59, 60, 61, 64
U.S. Army, p. 22 (bottom), 62 (left)
U.S. National Archives, p. 13 (bottom)
U.S. Navy, p. 30, 31, 41, 44, 46, 47, 50, 51, 55, 62 (right), 63

Copyright © 1970 by David C. Cooke

Trade ISBN 0-396-06203-2
Dodd Durable ISBN 0-396-06220-2

Library of Congress Catalog Card Number: 72-114237

Printed in the United States of America

FOREWORD

When World War II started on September 1, 1939, no nation in the world was truly prepared for hostilities. New aircraft types had been evolved on both sides, but none of these had been produced in any real quantity. History has proved that even Germany, which was then the strongest air power, had not prepared its factories for volume production of combat aircraft.

While Germany entered the war with a considerable numerical superiority in aircraft, it became obvious during the Battle of Britain that air power tactics by the generals had not kept pace with technological development in the factories. Thus, while the *Luftwaffe* had been overwhelmingly successful as an advance striking force for the German armies, it was soundly defeated by superior Royal Air Force tactics in the pure air power struggles over the British Isles.

Equally amazing, when the war ended, the Allies learned that our enemies had some of the most advanced airplanes ever conceived. A number of these machines, already in squadron service, were far more advanced than any aircraft the Allies had even in the planning stage.

The Germans had their first experimental jet plane flying as early as 1939. The first English jet was built in 1941, and the first one in the United States was not ready for flight testing until October 1, 1942. The Germans had a jet fighter ready for production in 1942, but the first successful jet fighter in the United States did not enter production until 1944.

The Germans and Japanese were also the first to develop rocket-propelled aircraft, a number of which were flown with operational squadrons. Today, with the war almost ancient history, no other nation has built rocket planes for anything other than test purposes.

The Germans and Japanese were the leaders in aviation technology at the beginning of the war and also at the end, when their cities and manufacturing facilities were in ruin as a result of Allied bombing. Even the Italians, who were so badly outclassed in the actual fighting, had developed airplanes which were superior to many of the Allied types which faced them.

The aircraft described on the following pages do not represent all the latest types built by our enemies during the war, but are those which were encountered most often in combat. The majority of them were worthy foes.

As a war correspondent, I saw a good number of these Axis airplanes flying overhead. I also heard the explosion of their bombs and the sound of their guns. I am thankful that I am still here to write about them.

DAVID C. COOKE

5

10140

For all the airmen—friend and foe.
Their courage cannot be questioned.

CONTENTS

CANT Z.501 GABBIANO

Forward section of the Z.501. The plane was made completely of wood, had two fuselage gun positions.

In the years between the two world wars the Italians concentrated a good portion of their aeronautical designing efforts on flying boats and seaplanes. This was because Italy is virtually surrounded by water and the leaders of the *Regia Aeronautica* assumed that in case of war they would be conducting most of their operations in the Adriatic, Tyrrhenian, or Ionian Seas, or perhaps down into the Mediterranean.

One of the finest Italian flying boats of this period was the Cant Z.501 Gabbiano (Gull), which was built by the Cantieri firm at Monfalcone. There was nothing graceful in the appearance of the airplane, but it was the finest flying boat of its type when it entered service in the fall of 1934.

One of the first Z.501's delivered by the factory proved its realiability on October 18-19, 1934, when it was flown by Mario Stoppani and a crew of two from Monfalcone to Massaua, Eritrea. This nonstop distance of 2,566 miles was a new international record for seaplanes. In July of the following year, another Z.501, again with Mario Stoppani at the controls, set a new duration mark when it flew nonstop for 3,063 miles.

The Z.501 was considered obsolete when Italy entered the war. However, there were still 15 operational squadrons equipped with some 200 of the machines. While these were poorly armed, mounting only four 7.7-millimeter machine guns, they were used throughout the war for patrol, reconnaissance, and light bombing. The plane's maximum bomb load was 1,400 pounds.

While there was no Z.501 construction during the war, a number of the planes were still in good flying condition when Italy surrendered. This was because their all-wood construction allowed them to absorb a tremendous amount of punishment without being destroyed.

Other data: Wing span, 73 feet 10 inches; length, 46 feet 11 inches; loaded weight, 15,510 pounds; engine, 850-horsepower Isotta-Fraschini Asso (Ace); maximum speed, 171 miles per hour at 8,200 feet.

The Gabbiano was slow and ungainly, but it could fly long distances and was useful for over-water patrol.

This is the Do.17V8, which was one of the original military test models. It carried no guns or bombs.

Because of its slim fuselage, the Do.17 was called the Flying Pencil. It was far advanced for its day.

DORNIER DO.17

Along with the Heinkel He.111 (page 18), the Do.17 was Germany's standard level bomber of the war. It was faster than the He.111, had a higher ceiling, and carried a larger bomb load, yet it was built in smaller numbers.

Also like the He.111, the Do.17 was originally designed as a passenger transport for Lufthansa Airlines. Three experimental models were built, the first of which was completed in the fall of 1934. After testing, Lufthansa decided that the plane would not be suitable for commercial operations

because of the cramped cabin. The following year the Air Ministry asked Dornier to produce a bomber version for the new *Luftwaffe*.

During tests with the Do.17V4 bomber, the Germans found that it was faster than most fighters. In July, 1937, a stripped-down version was demonstrated at a military aircraft competition in Zurich, Switzerland, and outdistanced the fastest single-seater at the meet, attaining a speed of 284 miles per hour.

As a further development, the Do.17 was given a bulbous nose, so that a gunner could be added to fire downward and to the rear. But the plane did not have enough protective firepower, and it was shot down in large numbers over England in 1940.

After further alterations, the designation was changed to Do.217, and the first production models were delivered in 1941. This was a much improved version, and an American expert called it "one of the best airplanes ever built."

Before bomber squadrons were supplied with the new models, a serious shortage of night fighters developed. The Do.217 was then produced as a fighter, carrying radar as well as four 20-millimeter cannon and four 7.9-millimeter machine guns.

Production of all Do.17 types was low. Available figures indicate that only about 1,730 Do.217's were supplied to operational squadrons. During the plane's production life the bomb load was increased from 1,760 pounds in the Do.17E to 8,820 pounds in the Do.217M. Its speed was also increased more than 125 miles per hour.

Other data (Do.217M-1): Wing span, 62 feet 4 inches; length, 55 feet 9 inches; loaded weight, 36,817 pounds; engines, two 1,750-horsepower Daimler-Benz; maximum speed, 348 miles per hour at 18,700 feet.

This Do.217 was captured virtually undamaged when the Allies took Italy's Castel Benito airfield in 1943.

The trimotored S.M.79 was rated by many Allied experts as the finest land-based torpedo-bomber of the war.

SAVOIA-MARCHETTI S.M.79

Italy was derided as being a second-class air power during the war, but this was far from the truth. In actual fact, it had several excellent airplanes, one of the best of which was the S.M.79 Sparviero (Hawk). Trimotored airplanes had gone out of vogue long before the S.M.79 was produced, yet this machine was rated by many authorities as the best land-based torpedo-bomber of the war. It was built in larger numbers than all other Italian multiengined aircraft combined.

The first S.M.79 appeared toward the end of 1934 as a commercial transport. On September 24, 1935, it established seven new records, including a speed of 245 miles per hour over a 625-mile course with a payload of 4,408 pounds. By the end of 1938, the airplane had set no less than 26 new international records.

When Italy entered World War II, the *Regia Aeronautica* had a total of 975 bombers, of which 594 were Sparvieros. The plane was extremely successful in combat. Among its other achievements, it sank a British aircraft carrier, at least five destroyers, and numerous cargo vessels.

The S.M.79's fuselage was of welded steel tube

construction with fabric covering, while the wing was made entirely of wood. It was capable of absorbing a tremendous amount of punishment and became known to Allied pilots as one of the most difficult planes to shoot down. Its normal load consisted of up to 2,750 pounds of bombs or torpedoes.

Other data (S.M.79-2): Wing span, 69 feet 7 inches; length, 53 feet 2 inches; loaded weight, 24,912 pounds; engines, three 1,000-horsepower Piaggios; maximum speed, 270 miles per hour at 12,000 feet.

Right: The reliable S.M.79 formed the backbone of Italy's offensive capabilities. *Below:* This is the first test model, which established 26 new records.

MESSERSCHMITT ME.109

In 1934, while all of the major powers of the world were still producing biplane fighters for their air forces, Willy Messerschmitt in Germany started design work on a single-seat low-wing airplane, which was later to achieve prominence as the *Luftwaffe's* standard first-line fighter. The first model was taken up for its initial tests in September, 1935.

The first production version of the Messerschmitt was the Me.109B-1, which first entered squadron

When war started, the Me.109 was the standard German fighter. It remained in production through 1944.

service in 1937. It had a 610-horsepower engine and a top speed of only 292 miles per hour with full military load. On November 11, 1937, however, a special racing model of the plane set a new world's speed record of 379.4 miles per hour. On April 26, 1939, another special version, the Me.209, boosted the speed record to 469.2 miles per hour. This mark still stands as the fastest speed ever achieved by a piston-powered airplane.

The first Me.109's to see war action were the B and D models, which participated in the Spanish Civil War of 1936-1937. The Me.109E entered production in 1939. This model had a maximum speed of 354 miles per hour.

The Me.109 was built in larger numbers than any other airplane in the war. According to official records, more than 33,000 of the fighters were delivered. However, mass production was not started until the war had been in progress for about three years. In 1940 monthly production was only 125. This was raised to 375 per month in 1941, 1,000 per month in 1943, and 2,500 per month in 1944.

During the war many Allied military experts insisted that the Me.109 was second-rate by comparison with various American and British types. General Henry H. Arnold, who was then Chief of the U.S. Army Air Forces, had a different opinion. He stated that the final production version of the Messerschmitt, the Me.109G, was the best fighter plane in the world for shooting down bombers.

Armament of the Me.109 was steadily improved. The first test model had only two 7.9-millimeter machine guns. By the time the Me.109G appeared in 1942, firepower had been increased to one 30-millimeter cannon, two 13-millimeter machine guns, and two 20-millimeter cannon.

Other data (Me.109G-10): Wing span, 32 feet 8 inches; length, 29 feet 4 inches; loaded weight, 7,700 pounds; engine, 1,800-horsepower Daimler-Benz; maximum speed, 428 miles per hour at 24,250 feet.

Right: A captured Me.109E in British markings. **Below:** Last production version was the fast Me.109G.

JUNKERS JU.87 STUKA

The Ju.87 Stuka was known early in the war as the most feared of all German warplanes. It was the airplane that dive bombed the Polish air force out of existence in a few days. It smashed solid Belgian fortresses in hours, and destroyed a mile-square section in the heart of Rotterdam, Holland. When the German armies swept into France, Ju.87's, flying in support of tanks, demoralized the French infantrymen and drove them into retreat. It was also because of the Stuka that Paris was declared an open city, so that it would be spared from devastation.

The Ju.87 had a truly amazing record, and it must go down in the record books as one of the most successful warplanes of all time. However, and just as amazing, it was not a particularly good airplane despite its successes. It was slow, awkward, poorly armed, and unable to combat determined aerial opposition. This became obvious during the Battle of Britain, when the Junkers dive bombers were shot down in large numbers by defending Hurricanes and Spitfires.

The Germans tried sending Messerschmitt fighters along to protect the Ju.87's. This was soon recognized as a waste of time, since the escorting

Three views of the Ju.87, which was one of the most successful warplanes of all time. However, it was poor in aerial combat, had weak defensive armament.

single-seaters were too fast to stay with the bombers. Because of continuing losses, all Stukas were finally withdrawn from operations over England.

The Ju.87 was developed from a plane that was obsolete by the time World War II began. This was the K-47, which the Junkers firm built in its Swedish factory in 1933. Two years later, when Hitler announced that he intended to build a new German air force, the K-47 was modified and redesignated Ju.87. The first model, the Ju.87V-1, was delivered in 1935. Ironically, this plane was powered by a British Rolls-Royce engine.

The Ju.87 was first combat-tested in the Spanish Civil War. The Germans were so excited by the performance of the plane, as well as the psychological effects of dive bombing, that it was ordered into quantity production.

The most heavily armed model of the Stuka was the Ju.87G, which had two 37-millimeter cannon plus two forward-firing 7.9-millimeter machine guns and two swivel 7.9-millimeter guns.

Other data (Ju.87D-1): Wing Span, 45 feet 3 inches; length, 37 feet 9 inches; loaded weight, 12,600 pounds; engine, 1,400-horsepower Junkers Jumo; maximum speed, 255 miles per hour at 13,500 feet.

The Ju.87 won fame as the dreaded Stuka, and it became one of the most talked-about German planes of the entire war. It had a top speed of only 255 m.p.h.

HEINKEL HE.111

The Heinkel He.111 earned many distinctions during its long operational career, the most dubious being that it was the German airplane which suffered most from Royal Air Force fighter pilots during the Battle of Britain in 1940.

Ernst Heinkel wrote in his autobiography, *He.1000*, that when he designed the He.111 he did not expect it to be anything other than a transport plane. The original model was built for Lufthansa, the German airline company, as a ten-passenger transport. When the plane first appeared in 1935, it was the fastest commercial transport in the world, with a speed of 255 miles per hour. The following year it was produced as the He.111B for the *Luftwaffe*, and in 1937 it was sent into action in the Spanish Civil War.

The He.111B was a resounding success in Spain. It was so fast that enemy fighters were unable to catch it. The Germans were so impressed that they ordered the machine into production as the *Luftwaffe's* standard high-level bomber.

The He.111 was very successful in attacks against Poland and France. However, its poor defensive armament and lack of armor plating made the plane virtually a "sitting duck" target for Hurricane and Spitfire pilots during the Battle of Britain. Despite this vulnerability, the He.111 was continued in production through 1944—primarily because the Germans did not develop a replacement.

In addition to normal service as a bomber, the plane was used to carry paratroopers, to lay mines, and as a torpedo bomber. As a bomber, it carried a maximum load of 5,510 pounds of bombs. The normal crew was five men.

Other data (He.111H-6): Wing span, 74 feet 1 inch; length, 54 feet 5 inches; loaded weight, 25,000 pounds; engines, two 1,340-horsepower Junkers Jumos; maximum speed, 258 miles per hour at 16,400 feet.

An He.111H being serviced prior to a mission. This photograph was taken in the early weeks of the war.

As an airplane, the He.111 was a technical success. However, it did not meet these same standards as a bomber. This was partly because of poor defensive armament and lack of protective armor for the crew.

CANT Z.506 AIRONE

Shortly after the appearance of their Z.501 Gabbiano flying boat in 1934 (page 8), the Italian firm of *Cantieri Riuniti dell'Adriatico* started design work on their Z-506 Airone (Heron). When the first test model was rolled from the factory in 1936, foreign observers considered it unusual for several reasons. One of these was its trimotor configuration, which most countries had long since discontinued; another was its all-wood construction, since by that time most aircraft were being made entirely of metal, generally aluminum alloy.

While the Z.506 was originally designed as a landplane for commercial transportation with Ala Littoria, the Italian airline, the Air Ministry also requested that the machine be mounted on twin floats for military purposes.

As a landplane, the Z.506 was an instant success. It established no less than 16 new international records. Eleven of these were for speed with various loads ranging up to 11,923 pounds, three were for distance over closed courses, and two were for altitude with designated payloads. The longest of the closed-circuit flights was 3,231 miles.

The seaplane version ordered by the *Regia Aeronautica* continued to make records. One of these was a flight from Cádiz, Spain, across the South Atlantic Ocean to Caravelas, Brazil—a distance of 4,326 miles.

In 1938 the Cantieri firm produced a larger and faster development of the Airone. This was called the Z.509, but it was basically similar to the earlier model. In one flight on March 30, 1938, a Z.509 set eight new world's records. But despite the improved performance of the newer plane, it was not produced for military purposes.

The Z.506 was the largest and finest marine-based airplane in service with the Italians during the war. It was also one of the largest airplanes anywhere in the world that had ever been mounted on twin floats for water operations.

The Airone had a normal crew of five. It was poorly defended, with only three 7.7-millimeter machine guns and one 12.7-millimeter gun. Its bomb load consisted of up to 2,645 pounds of bombs or torpedoes. This explosive load was carried internally, though provisions were made on some aircraft to mount small bombs on wing racks.

The Z.506 was vulnerable to attack because of its low speed. However, it scored a number of successes at low altitude against Allied shipping. Several of the planes survived the war and remained in active service on air-sea rescue duty until near the end of 1959.

Other data (Z.506B): Wing span, 86 feet 11 inches; length, 63 feet 4 inches; loaded weight, 28,008 pounds; engines, three 770-horsepower Alfa Romeos; maximum speed, 217 miles per hour at 12,120 feet.

The Z.506 Airone was the largest and finest marine-based airplane in service with the Italians. Some of the many records it established before the war remained unbeaten by modern types for some 20 years.

Above: This Me.110 was captured in North Africa. It had been under service when the airfield was over-run. *Below:* An Me.110 with radar for night fighting.

MESSERSCHMITT ME.110

Willy Messerschmitt's Me.110 was an unusual concept when it was designed in 1934. Until that time, all fighters had been fairly small and with single engines. The Me.110 was the world's first twin-engined, all-metal, low-wing fighter. The experimental model was taken up for its first test flights on May 12, 1936, and it was an instant success. By comparison, the first twin-engined fighter built in the United States, the Lockheed P-38 Lightning, was not flown for the first time until January 12, 1939.

The following month the XP-38 was destroyed in a crash landing.

The idea of the Me.110 was similar to that of the Bristol Fighter of World War I. Messerschmitt envisioned a fast, maneuverable fighter with the added advantage of a rear gunner. But the plane never achieved the distinction of the Bristol, mostly because of official interference.

In 1938 Hermann Goering started to create special "destroyer" squadrons of Me.110's. These units were supposed to become the operational elite of the *Luftwaffe* to protect Germany from enemy bombers. However, the plan was discontinued, and the Me.110 turned into a so-called intruder-bomber, following the reverses in the Battle of Britain. In its bomber version, the plane carried a normal bomb load of 1,400 pounds.

When airborne radar was finally developed by the Germans, the Me.110 was turned into a night fighter, and it proved highly successful against Royal Air Force bombers. But rather than keeping the plane in this effective role, the Germans started building it once again as a bomber.

Other data (Me.110G-4): Wing span, 53 feet 5 inches; length, 41 feet 7 inches; loaded weight, 20,700 pounds; engines, two 1,475-horsepower Daimler-Benz; maximum speed, 342 miles per hour at 22,900 feet.

A captured Me.110 with R.A.F. markings. The plane was fast but could not match most Allied single-seaters.

FIAT B.R.20 CICOGNA

When the Fiat B.R.20 Cicogna (Stork) first appeared in 1936, it was one of the finest and fastest bombers then flying. It carried a bomb load of 3,520 pounds, and with its four 7.7-millimeter defensive machine guns it was considered a dangerous machine to attack.

The plane was not immediately ordered into quantity production. First, a contingent was sent to

Last production version of the Cicogna was the B.R. 20*bis*, which was improved over the earlier models.

Spain for combat testing with General Francisco Franco's forces. These proved formidable in battle and capable of fending off attacks by Russian fighters in service with the Loyalists. Following this experience, limited production was ordered for the *Regia Aeronautica*. Eighty of the machines were also exported to Japan during 1938.

The Italians could have used the aircraft they

sold to their Asian Axis partner, for only about 150 B.R.20's were in squadron service when Italy entered the war. These were first used in limited operations in the southern part of France, mostly in nuisance raids to keep French fighters away from the main battle zone in the north.

After the fall of France, about 75 B.R.20's were flown to Brussels, Belgium, for night bombing raids against England in support of the German *Luftwaffe*. Casualties were high, since the Italian machine was no match for defending Hawker Hurricanes and Supermarine Spitfires. After three months the surviving planes were withdrawn and returned to Italy, to support the invasion of Greece.

After the conquest of Greece had been completed and there was no necessity for further bombing missions, several squadrons of Cicognas were dispatched to the Russian Front. However, some were stationed in Italy, where they ranged over the Mediterranean to bomb Allied merchant vessels and warships.

Well before the end of the war the B.R.20 was considered "easy meat" for Allied fighter pilots. Although about 600 of the machines entered squadron service, only a few of these still remained at the end of Italy's participation in the war.

Other data (B.R.20M): Wing span, 70 feet 9 inches; length, 53 feet; loaded weight, 22,220 pounds; engines, two 1,000-horsepower Fiat A.80R.-C.41's; maximum speed, 256 miles per hour at 15,448 feet.

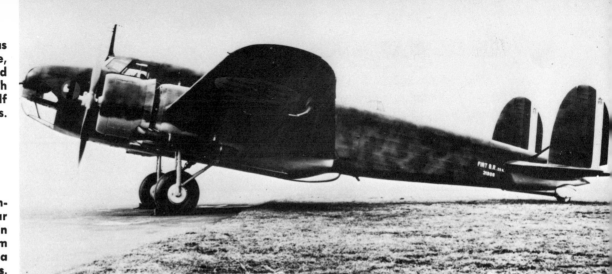

Right: The B.R.20M was an attractive machine, but it was underpowered and did not have enough guns to defend itself properly from fighters.

Below: The plane's general lines were similar to the American Martin B-10. It had a maximum speed of 256 m.p.h., a range of 1,860 miles.

JUNKERS JU.88

There is no question that the Ju.88 was one of the truly outstanding airplanes on either side during the war. Allied experts acknowledged this by calling the machine "ingenious" and "one of the best all-around airplanes in existence."

The design was conceived in 1935 in response to an official request for a high-speed medium bomber, and the first test model was completed late in December the following year. The Germans were so enthusiastic over the performance of the airplane that a fighter version was also ordered. This was ready

Right: Part of a Ju.88's cockpit. It had excellent instrumentation for the pilot. *Below*: The Ju.88A-13 was used for ground attack, carried up to 16 guns.

on September 27, 1938, which was well before the first production bombers left the assembly line at the Junkers factory in Bernburg.

The Ju.88 was outstanding in all respects. In March, 1939, Ernst Siebert set a world's record in a Ju.88 by flying 620 miles with a payload of 4,400 pounds at an average speed of 321.2 miles per hour. Two months later Siebert established another record by flying 1,240 miles at 311 miles per hour.

The Germans had considerable difficulty in getting the Ju.88 into production, which was one of the reasons they lost the Battle of Britain. But when the plane was available in sufficient numbers as a fighter, it became a potent weapon. Royal Air Force bombers lost so heavily to Ju.88 night fighters that the Air Ministry came close to calling off all such nighttime operations.

The Ju.88 was in production throughout the war. A total of about 13,000 of the machines was built, some 4,000 of which were fighters. However, the plane entered volume production too late to give the *Luftwaffe* a real advantage in the air war. The final version of the basic design was the Ju.388, only a few of which were produced before the end of the war. The Ju.388 had a speed of 462 miles per hour.

Other data (Ju.88G-7): Wing span, 65 feet 10 inches; length, 54 feet 1 inch; loaded weight, 32,350 pounds, engines, two 1,880-horsepower Junkers Jumos; maximum speed, 363 miles per hour at 33,500 feet.

Last production version was the Ju.388K-1 bomber, which did not see active service. It could do 362 m.p.h.

A captured G.50 in Libya. The Italians damaged the tail so the plane could not be flown against them.

FIAT G.50 FRECCIA

The Fiat G.50 Freccia (Arrow) was the first modern low-wing, all-metal fighter built in Italy. When it was first flown on February 26, 1937, the plane was far ahead of any single-seat fighter in service or in the experimental stage in the United States. The first test model performed so well that a small production order was given. Some of these were sent to Spain for combat testing against the Loyalists.

While the G.50 established a good record in Spain against Russian Polikarpov I-15 biplanes and I-16 monoplanes, it was obviously underpowered and incapable of performing as well as the general design seemed to indicate.

When Italy entered World War II, the G.50 was the only low-wing fighter that had been delivered to the *Regia Aeronautica* in any appreciable numbers. Along with the C.R.42 biplane (page 38) the G.50 was forced to bear the brunt of aerial warfare over Greece and Albania through February, 1941. But while the G.50 was more maneuverable than its Allied adversaries, it did not have sufficient speed or firepower. Normal armament was only two 12.7-millimeter machine guns, though later models also had two 7.7-millimeter guns in the wings.

The G.50 continued as a second best for most of its operational life. Then in 1942 it was fitted with an Italian-built version of the German Daimler-Benz liquid-cooled engine—and suddenly the airplane became one of the very best single-seat fighters of the war.

The new version was designated G.55 Centauro (Centaur). It not only retained the maneuverability of earlier models but had a speed of 385 miles per hour. One American pilot said he would rather fight a Messerschmitt Me.109 any time than a G.55. The last plane in the series was the G.56, which had a 1,750-horsepower Daimler-Benz engine and a maximum speed of 426 miles per hour. Italy surrendered before this model could be put into production.

Other data (G.55): Wing span, 38 feet 10 inches; length, 30 feet 9 inches; loaded weight, 8,179 pounds; engine, 1,475-horsepower Fiat R.A.1050; maximum speed, 385 miles per hour at 22,965 feet.

Above: Many G.50's were captured during the North African campaign. Most had been grounded through lack of spare parts. *Below:* The last production version was the G.55, which had a speed of 385 m.p.h.

AICHI D3A

When the Japanese struck at Pearl Harbor, Hawaii, on December 7, 1941, the attack was spearheaded by Aichi D3A dive bombers. The plane was built by the Aichi Clock and Electric Machine Company, and it became one of the most successful of all airplanes in the Imperial Japanese Navy, generally operating from aircraft carriers.

The day after the attack on Pearl Harbor, Aichis also led a strike against the British base at Singapore. After another two days they joined Mitsubishi bombers in an attack against British warships off the coast of Malaya.

The Aichi dive bombers continued to score heavily. On June 5, 1942, during the Battle of Midway, they damaged the American aircraft carrier *Yorktown* so severely that on the following day it was easy prey for a Japanese submarine and was sent to the bottom. Four months later two Aichis destroyed the American carrier *Hornet*.

The D3A scored tremendous successes despite the fact that it was slow, poorly armed, and had neither self-sealing fuel tanks nor armor plate. Normal arm-

While the D3A was slow and poorly armed, and with little protection for the crew, it was very successful.

A wartime picture of an Aichi dive bomber going out an a mission. It was highly maneuverable without bombs.

ament was two 7.7-millimeter forward-firing guns and one swivel gun. The maximum bomb load was 1,050 pounds.

The D3A was designed in 1936, following a careful study of German dive bombers, including various Heinkel models. The first version was designated D3A1, and it was flight-tested in the early spring of 1937. The Japanese Navy's evaluation team was highly pleased with the performance of the machine, and it was ordered into immediate production. That same year, in December, service models started going into squadron operation, first from land bases for pilot familiarization and then from aircraft carriers in simulated wartime operations.

The D3A1 was the first all-metal, low-wing dive bomber built for the Japanese Navy. A total of 478 of the planes was delivered before it was altered to become the D3A2. Among other changes, the new version had a more powerful engine, which resulted in better performance. Production of D3A2 types was 1,016. In the Japanese Navy both versions were known as Type 99 carrier dive bombers. They remained in service throughout the war.

Other data (D3A2): Wing span, 47 feet 7 inches; length, 34 feet 9 inches; loaded weight, 9,347 pounds; engine, 1,030-horsepower Mitsubishi Kinsei (Golden Star); maximum speed, 266 miles per hour at 18,536 feet.

MITSUBISHI KI.21

When the Mitsubishi Ki.21 heavy bomber first entered service toward the end of 1937, it was not only the best bomber in the Japanese Army Air Force but one of the best twin-engined bombers flying anywhere in the world. Although the machine was outmoded before the end of the war, it continued to remain in action as the backbone of Japanese Army offensive operations throughout the Pacific theatre.

One of the reasons for the long service life of the machine was that it was built to the most exacting Japanese Army specifications ever issued. These specifications were released to aircraft manufacturers in February, 1936, and they called for a bomber capable of flying long distances, a maximum speed of 250 miles per hour at 10,000 feet, and the ability to carry a bomb load of 1,650 pounds for five hours at a cruising speed of 190 miles per hour. Only two manufacturers entered aircraft in the competition—Nakajima and Mitsubishi. The Mitsubishi design won by a wide margin. It not only met all of the requirements but exceeded some of them.

The company completed five experimental models of the Ki.21 in the spring of 1937, each with various armament arrangements. The military decided upon the version with three 7.7-millimeter machine guns. Armament was later increased to five 7.7-millimeter guns and one 12.7-millimeter gun. The bomb load was also increased from 1,650 pounds to 2,200 pounds. When production of the plane was discontinued in September, 1944, a total of 2,054 had been delivered.

While the Ki.21 was totally outclassed by the time production came to an end, it was the most famous Japanese bomber of the war. Prior to the war, it fought in China and against the Russians and turned Japan into the strongest offensive air power in the Far East.

Other data (Ki.21-2B): Wing span, 72 feet 10 inches; length, 52 feet 6 inches; loaded weight, 21,407 pounds; engines, two 1,490-horsepower Mitsubishi Ha.101's; maximum speed, 297 miles per hour at 12,120 feet.

A flight of Ki.21's starting to drop their load of bombs. This photo is from a captured combat movie.

A bombing mission over China prior to Japan's entry into the war. The Ki.21 had a top speed of 297 m.p.h.

The C.200 was one of the best Italian single-seaters. Poor firepower prevented it from being outstanding.

MACCHI C.200 SAETTA

The Italian Macchi C.200 Saetta (Lightning), like the British Supermarine Spitfire, was developed from a record-breaking seaplane racer. In the case of the Spitfire, the progenitor was the S.6, which in 1931 set a new world's speed record of 407.5 miles per hour. The Macchi M.C.72 was considerably faster, raising the international mark to 440.6 miles per hour in 1934.

The C.200, like the earlier M.C.72, was designed by Mario Castoldi, who was one of Italy's finest aeronautical engineers. The experimental model was taken up for its first flight on December 24, 1937. The following year Macchi received a contract for 99 production versions. When Italy entered the war, only 196 of the fighters had been delivered and another 572 were on order.

Combat proved that the Saetta was slightly slower than the Hawker Hurricane but could climb, dive, and maneuver better. However, armament was not heavy enough. The first models had only two 12.7-millimeter machine guns synchronized to fire through the propeller arc; this was later augmented by two 7.7-millimeter guns in the wings.

The plane's record on the Eastern Front was far better. Two squadrons of C.200's were credited with 88 Russian aircraft destroyed with a loss to themselves of only 15.

Despite its excellent potentials, the Saetta was never built in quantity. A total of only about 1,000 of the fighters was delivered.

Other data (C.200-11): Wing span, 34 feet 9 inches; length, 26 feet 10 inches; loaded weight, 5,121 pounds; engine, 840-horsepower Fiat; maximum speed, 312 miles per hour at 14,760 feet.

Above: The clean lines of the Saetta are obvious in this picture. The pilot had good visibility. *Below:* C.200 pilots practice formation flying over Italy.

KAWASAKI KI.45 TORYU

Well before the outbreak of World War II in Europe, the Japanese realized that their Army Air Force would require a long-range twin-engined fighter for operations over the Pacific Ocean. The Ki.45 Toryu (Dragon Killer) was the result. The design was started in 1937 under the designation Ki.38, and the first test models were delivered in January, 1939. So many alterations were required, however, that the plane was redesignated Ki.45. Because of the numerous design changes, production could not be started until September, 1941.

While the Toryu was originally planned for long-range operations, it became most successful as a night fighter in defense of the Japanese homeland. The plane went into operation against raiding Boeing B-29 Superfortresses for the first time on June 15, 1944. According to official Japanese records, the eight Ki.45 interceptors destroyed seven of the attacking B-29's and probably destroyed three others. Similar successes were claimed against later Superfortress missions.

The plane was fitted with a variety of armament

The K.45 was originally designed as a long-range escort fighter. It was later adapted as a night fighter.

arrangements. Normal armament was one 20-millimeter cannon and two 12.7-millimeter guns for the pilot and one 7.9-millimeter gun in the rear cockpit. Another version had three cannon—two 20-millimeter and one 37-millimeter. Yet another had a 75-millimeter cannon for attacks against shipping.

Total production amounted to 1,698. These were widely used throughout the Southwest Pacific. Some were also employed in suicide attacks against Allied warships.

Other data (Ki.45-KAIC): Wing span, 49 feet 5 inches; length, 36 feet 1 inch; loaded weight, 12,125 pounds; engines, two 1,080-horsepower Mitsubishi Ha.102's; maximum speed, 340 miles per hour at 22,965 feet.

Above: The Ki.45-KAIC had one forward-firing cannon and two machine guns. **Below:** A line-up of captured Toryus. The planes were maneuverable for their size.

FIAT C.R.42 FALCO

When the war started in 1939, all of the major world powers still had biplanes serving with their air forces. The British had the Gloster Gladiator and Fairey Swordfish, the Germans had various Arados and Henschels, and Grumman was still building its F3F-3 single-seat fighter for the U.S. Navy. In Italy, the Fiat firm had just started building the attractive C.R.42 Falco (Falcon). The plane was continued in production until late 1942, thus becoming the last of the biplane fighters.

The heritage of the C.R.42 can be traced back to the Ansaldo SVA fighters, which were the most notable single-seaters produced by the Italians during World War I. The Ansaldo firm became part of the Fiat complex in March, 1926, and a short time later they produced the C.R.30. This machine was essentially a cleaned-up, higher-powered version of the old SVA-5, using virtually the same wing bracing system.

This basic design was continued through four further series of fighters. Then Celestino Rosatelli, chief engineer for Fiat, completed his C.R.42 early in 1939.

The Italians had allowed their *Regia Aeronautica* to deteriorate badly, and they had drafted a plan to modernize. This was called the R Plan, and it provided for building 3,000 new warplanes, mostly fighters, in the shortest possible time. One of the

types selected for construction was the C.R.42.

When the Italians entered the war they had more Falcos than any other fighter. These were exceptionally maneuverable, and they established good records against the Gloster Gladiators in Greece and Albania. However, experience in North Africa proved that maneuverability alone was no match for higher speed and heavier firepower.

While the C.R.42's did not fare well against more modern Royal Air Force fighters, the Italian pilots

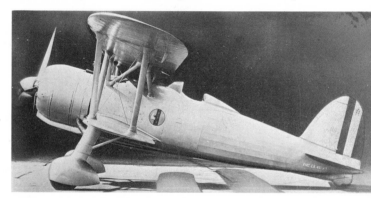

Two views of the C.R.42, which was the last and the finest of the Italian single-seat biplane fighters.

A captured Falco in North Africa. The plane was slow by World War II standards, but its pilots liked it.

complained when their biplanes were replaced with monoplanes.

The C.R.42 was built in larger numbers than any other Italian fighter of the war. A total of 1,781 of the machines left the production lines. Original armament consisted of two 12.7- millimeter machine guns, but later models also had two 7.7-millimeter guns in the wings.

Other data: Wing span, 31 feet 9 inches; length, 27 feet 1 inch; loaded weight, 5,049 pounds; engine, 840-horsepower Fiat; maximum speed, 274 miles per hour at 20,000 feet.

A captured Zero with Chinese markings. The machine outflew Curtiss P-40's used by the Flying Tigers.

Wing tips of the A6M2-21 folded for stowage aboard aircraft carriers. It had a top speed of 332 m.p.h.

MITSUBISHI A6M

When design engineer Jiro Horikoshi of the Mitsubishi company first saw the performance specifications of the new single-seat fighter desired by the Japanese Navy, he felt that these would be impossible to meet. Each of the demands was for performance far in excess of any fighter then flying anywhere in the world. The year was 1937, and the fighter the Japanese Navy wanted was finally to emerge as the Type 0, or Zero, which became the most famous Japanese airplane of World War II.

When the test program began with the first A6M1's on April 1, 1939, the plane was the finest shipboard fighter in existence. It was also superior to the land-based Messerschmitt Me.109E as well as the existing models of the Hawker Hurricane and Supermarine Spitfire. The best fighter in the United

States was the Curtiss P-40 Hawk, and this machine, while more rugged, could not match any of the Zero's performance characteristics.

Fifteen Zeros were sent to China in the summer of 1940 for combat testing, and they were not only faster but more maneuverable than any of the defending fighters. General Claire Chennault, commander of the American Volunteer Group in China, which became famous as the Flying Tigers, tried to warn the U.S. Army Air Forces about the Zero. However, his warning was ignored and the plane came as a complete surprise to American airmen when it was first encountered in combat.

For two years the Zero remained the finest fighter in the Pacific, outflying and outfighting most American opposition. When the Grumman F6F Hellcat and North American P-51 Mustang went into action, however, the Zero lost its superiority.

An A6M3-32 being tested by the U.S. Navy. This model mounted two 7.7-mm. guns and two 20-mm. cannon.

All of Japan's top aces flew the Mitsubishi A6M. The highest-ranking of these was Hiroyoshi Nishizwa, who scored 103 confirmed victories. Another ace, Saburo Sakai, used a Zero to shoot down six Boeing B-17 Flying Fortresses in a single fight.

The Zero was built in larger numbers than any other Japanese plane. While there were less than 500 in service when Pearl Harbor was attacked, total production amounted to 10,938.

Other data (A6M3-53C): Wing span, 36 feet 1 inch; length, 29 feet 9 inches; loaded weight, 6,047 pounds; engine, 1,130-horsepower Nakajima Sakae (Prosperity); maximum speed, 346 miles per hour at 19,680 feet.

The three photos on the right show the clean design of the Zero. Inspection and tests of captured craft proved that it was a fine design in most respects.

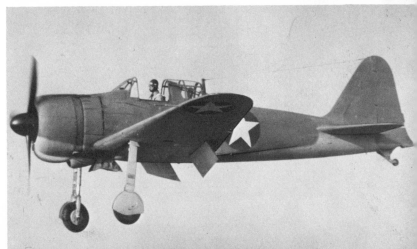

41

There is no question that the Fw.190 was one of the finest fighters built by any nation during the war.

An Fw.190 on a German airfield. The Allies destroyed more Focke-Wulfs on the ground than in the air.

FOCKE-WULF FW.190

The Fw.190 was clearly the very best propeller-driven single-seat fighter produced by the Germans during the entire course of the war. It was not only considerably faster than the Supermarine Spitfire, but could outfly and outfight its Royal Air Force rival at any altitude between 11,000 and 20,000 feet. Beyond this latter height, however, its performance fell off sharply.

The Focke-Wulf fighter was designed in 1938 and the first experimental model was tested on June 1 the following year. During these trials it achieved a speed of 370 miles per hour, making it the fastest single-seater in the world. Hermann Goering saw the machine for the first time early in 1940, and he was so impressed that he said, "We must turn these new fighters out like so many hot rolls!" Fortunately for the Allies, this type of production was never achieved and the plane was given second place in priority to the Messerschmitt Me.109.

When Fw-190's were flown into combat for the first time in July, 1941, they were a shock to the British. Here was an airplane that could not only beat the Spitfire in a fight but could run away from it if necessary. The Royal Air Force was not able to match the Fw.190 for two years. However, the Germans did not have enough of the planes to win true aerial superiority. *Luftwaffe* fighter pilots constantly demanded Fw.190's as replacements for their

Me.109's, but these did not come through quickly enough.

In its original form, the Fw.190 had a radial engine—the first modern German fighter to mount such an engine—and four machine guns. Armament was later increased to four 20-millimeter cannon and two 13-millimeter machine guns.

The final development of the plane was the Ta.152, which had a speed of 463 miles per hour at 34,000 feet. This was the fastest speed achieved by any propeller-driven fighter of the war.

Other data (Fw.190A-8): Wing span, 34 feet 5 inches; length, 29 feet; loaded weight, 9,750 pounds; engine, 1,700-horsepower B.M.W.; maximum speed, 408 miles per hour at 20,600 feet.

Above: The Fw.190 had an unusually long landing gear so it could swing its large propeller. *Below:* Final version of the plane was the extremely fast Ta.152.

MITSUBISHI G4M

When the first Mitsubishi G4M was captured intact by the U.S. Navy and taken up for an evaluation test, the pilot reported that it was one of the finest planes of its type he had ever flown, with performance characteristics comparable to the best American twin-engined bombers.

The Mitsubishi design was one of the most versatile airplanes ever developed for the Japanese Navy, which identified the machine merely as the Type 1. In addition to its normal role as a level bomber, it was used for torpedo-bombing, photo-reconnaissance, and even night fighting.

Engineering work was completed by Mitsubishi in 1938, and the first G4M1 was ready for testing in October, 1939. Because of various delays, less than 200 of the planes had been delivered by the time Japan entered the war.

The bomber was very successful in its first operations and scored some of the most important Japanese victories. During the first few days of the Pacific war Mitsubishi located the British battleship *Prince of Wales* and the cruiser *Repulse* and sank both of them. This cleared the way for Japanese invasion of Malaya and the East Indies.

The first production model of the Mitsubishi was called the G4M1. The improved G4M2 appeared in 1942. This model had more powerful engines, better armament, and a longer range. While the plane was designed to operate from land bases, it was flown from aircraft carriers during the Battle of Midway.

An excellent airplane, the G4M was comparable to the best medium bomber any of the Allies had in the war.

Though the Mitsubishi bomber was developed for the Japanese Navy, it was usually flown from land bases.

A G4M at the airfield in Hokkaido, Japan, its propellers removed in accordance with surrender terms.

G4M2's were also used to carry jet- and rocket-propelled suicide planes to within a few miles of their objectives, where they were dropped to continue their flight alone.

Total G4M production was 2,479. While the plane was excellent, losses were high because of poor armor plate and lack of self-sealing fuel tanks.

Other data (G4M2A): Wing span, 81 feet 8 inches; length, 64 feet 5 inches: loaded weight, 27,557 pounds; engines, two 1,850-horsepower Mitsubishi Kasei (Mars); maximum speed, 272 miles per hour at 15,090 feet.

With its landing gear up, the G4M was smoothly streamlined. Its bombs or torpedoes were in the fuselage.

While the Ki.46 did not seem to be unusual, it was called "one of the most perfect airplanes" ever built.

MITSUBISHI KI.46

Practically every airplane has problems of some sort. This is why many different models are often made, in an effort to eliminate various difficulties and also increase performance. The Mitsubishi Ki.46 was virtually a fault-free airplane and was called "one of the most perfect machines produced by any of the combatants in the war."

The Ki.46 was designed in 1938 as a command reconnaissance plane, and the first model was ready in November, 1939. Its performance was even better than the designers had anticipated. With two engines rated at only 850 horsepower each, it had a maximum speed of 312 miles per hour and could

flip and turn with the agility of a single-seater.

The first production model was the Ki.46-2, with 1,050-horsepower engines. This boost in power increased the plane's speed more than 50 miles per hour.

Combat experience proved that the Ki.46-2 had so much better performance than the Allied fighters it encountered that the machine gun in the rear cockpit was removed as unnecessary. The plane was so fast that American fighters were unable to intercept it, and its service ceiling of 35,170 feet was higher than most U.S. Navy planes could fly.

The Ki.46 was such a superior airplane that a German technical mission in Japan recommended that it be built for the *Luftwaffe* under license. The recommendation was dropped only because the Germans had decided to proceed with their development of jet-propelled types.

Though the Mitsubishi Ki.46 had been designed strictly for observation purposes, one version was produced as a fighter to intercept Boeing B-29 Superfortresses. This was designated the Ki.46-3-Kai, and it had one 37-millimeter cannon plus two 20-millimeter cannon or two 12.7-millimeter machine guns. Maximum speed was 397 miles per hour.

In addition to its excellent speed and performance, the Ki.46 could fly farther than most Japanese planes. The Ki.46-2 had a range of 1,535 miles, but this was increased to 2,485 miles in the Ki.46-3. Production of all versions was 1,738.

Other data (Ki.46-2): Wing span, 48 feet 3 inches; length, 36 feet 1 inch; loaded weight, 11,133 pounds; engines, two 1,050-horsepower Mitsubishi Ha.102's; maximum speed, 375 miles per hour at 19,000 feet.

The Ki.46 was so speedy that American fighters could not intercept it. Its service ceiling was 35,170 feet.

MACCHI C.202 FOLGORE

While the Macchi C.202 Folgore (Thunderbolt) was actually an improved version of the C.200 Saetta (page 34), the plane deserves individual description because it proved even more successful than its predecessor.

When Mario Castoldi designed the C.200 he had wanted to power it with an in-line engine, but since no such engines of sufficient power were then being manufactured in Italy, he was forced to use the Fiat radial. The efficient and more powerful German Daimler-Benz liquid-cooled engine was finally made available in 1940, and one of these was installed in a C.200. The plane was ready for testing on August 10 of the same year, and its performance excited the Italian military.

The Daimler-Benz engine was placed in production by Alfa Romeo as the Monsoni (Monsoon), and necessary alterations were made in C.200 plans so that the plane could be continued on the assembly line as the C.202.

Folgores started reaching service squadrons late in 1941, and they were immediately successful. The plane could outmaneuver all Allied fighters it encountered and could climb better than any of its adversaries with the exception of the Supermarine Spitfire.

A captured Folgore was tested by the U.S. Army Air Forces and, after landing, the pilot called it "a honey of an airplane." But despite the machine's superior performance, it could not be built in quantity because of slow engine deliveries. Total production was only about 1,500.

The last production model of the basic design was the C.205V Veltro (Greyhound), which was flown for the first time on April 19, 1942. It had a maximum speed of 399 miles per hour. Only 262 of these were built before Italy surrendered.

Other data (C.202-11): Wing span, 34 feet 9 inches; length, 29 feet; loaded weight, 6,459 pounds; engine, 1,175-horsepower Alfa Romeo Monsoni; maximum speed, 369 miles per hour at 17,056 feet.

With an Italian version of the German Daimler-Benz engine, the C.202 was outstanding in every respect.

Above: British soldiers look over a C.202 that made a wheels-up landing in Libya. There is no sign of battle damage to the enemy plane.

Below: Last version of design was the C.205, which had a top speed of 399 m.p.h. This model barely got into assembly-line production.

KAWANISHI H8K

While the Japanese spent a great amount of time and money prior to the war to build a powerful fleet of warships and aircraft carriers, it seems strange that they did not concentrate more effort on designing and building flying boats. When the war started the only large flying boat in service was the Kawanishi H6K, which was the first four-engined airplane ever built in Japan. But while the H6K was dependable and had a range of 3,107 miles, it was slow and vulnerable to attack.

The H8K was designed as a replacement for the earlier H6K, with a 30 per cent increase in speed and a 50 per cent increase in range. The first model was completed in December, 1940, and tests proved it to be a fine machine with excellent performance and handling characteristics. The H8K was not only the best flying boat ever built in Japan, it was also the fastest and most maneuverable aircraft of its

The large Kawanishi H8K was the fastest patrol-bomber used by any of the major powers engaged in the war.

Graceful in flight, the H8K had a longer range than other Japanese planes. The usual crew was ten men.

This remarkable photograph shows an H8K going down, one of its engines blazing from U.S. Navy bullets.

type to see service with any country involved in the war.

H8K's saw their first war action in March, 1942, during an attack against Oahu in the Hawaiian Islands. Following this they were in service throughout the Pacific. They were used for long-range patrol, bombing, torpedo-bombing, and for transportation of troops and supplies. Defensive armament was five 20-millimeter cannon and four 7.7-millimeter machine guns. It had a cruising range of 4,370 miles and could carry a bomb load of 4,410 pounds. Normal crew consisted of ten men.

Following the war, comparison tests were made between an H8K and a U.S. Navy Consolidated PB2Y-2 Coronado, which was similar in general layout. The Japanese plane was not only 70 miles per hour faster but had a longer range and could carry a heavier load.

The H8K was not built in quantity, mostly because of the demand for smaller combat types. Total production was only 167. An unarmed transport version called the Seiku (Clear Sky) was also produced in small numbers.

Other data (H8K2): Wing span, 124 feet 7 inches; length, 92 feet 3 inches; loaded weight, 54,013 pounds; engines, four 1,850-horsepower Mitsubishi Kasei (Mars); maximum speed, 283 miles per hour at 15,485 feet.

MESSERSCHMITT ME.163 KOMET

The Messerschmitt Me.163 Komet (Comet) earned the distinction of being the world's first operational rocket-propelled airplane. It was also the first airplane ever built capable of exceeding 600 miles per hour in level flight.

When an experimental model of the machine was taken up for its first flights in the spring of 1941, Heini Dittmar, the test pilot, slowly pushed the speed higher and higher. Finally, on May 10, he attained a speed of 601 miles per hour. At that time the official world's record for landplanes was only 469.2 miles per hour. This had been set by the Me.209.

The Me.163 actually dated back to an experimental tailless glider built in 1932—seven years before the outbreak of war. Wind-tunnel tests indicated that with a rocket engine with a thrust of 1,650 pounds, the plane would be able to reach a speed of 620 miles per hour. However, the first Komet was completed before the engine was available. While waiting for its engine, the plane was flown first as a glider and then with an 85-horsepower Argus engine in the nose.

When the first engines finally arrived from the Helmut Walter plant, they were found to be unde-

Messerschmitt's Me.163 in various stages of development. The two photos above are of experimental versions, while the bottom view shows a combat model.

pendable and dangerous. If a pilot landed with even a small amount of fuel remaining in his tanks, there was a chance that the ship would explode.

After numerous other problems and official delays, the Komet was put into production in 1944. A total of 327 planes left the assembly line that year, but only 37 were produced in 1945. This reduced production was due to the efficiency of Allied bombing raids.

In its first operations against American bombers, the Komets were so successful that U.S. Army Air Force leaders became alarmed. This was one of the main reasons for the order to intensify attacks against German aircraft factories.

One Me.163 was sent to Japan by submarine. However, the sub was sunk. Despite this, the Japanese produced their own version from factory plans. This was the Mitsubishi J8M1 Shusui (Rush of Wind).

Other data (Me.163B-1): Wing span, 30 feet 7 inches; length, 18 feet 8 inches, loaded weight, 9,500 pounds; engine, 3,750-pounds-thrust Walter HWK rocket; maximum speed, 596 miles per hour at 30,000 feet.

A captured Me.163. Germany was the only country ever to develop and build a rocket-powered combat airplane.

The Ki.61 was a surprise to the Allies when it first went into action. It was superior to the Grumman F6F.

KAWASAKI KI.61 HIEN

There is no question but that the Kawasaki Ki.61 Hien (Flying Swallow) was the best liquid-cooled, single-seat fighter produced for the Japanese Army Air Force during the war. When it was first encountered in combat, Allied pilots were sure that the plane was a Japanese version of the German Messerschmitt Me.109. However, the Ki.61 was a completely original design, and it actually resembled the P-51 Mustang more than the Messerschmitt.

While the Ki.61 owed nothing to the Me.109 except perhaps design inspiration, it was powered by a Japanese version of the Daimler-Benz engine built under license. Manufacturing rights for the German engine had been procured as early as 1937. Design work on the airplane itself was started in February, 1940, and the first test models were ready in December, 1941.

When the Hien first went into action it was a complete surprise to the Allies. The plane was not only as fast as those it faced in battle but had heavy armament, self-sealing fuel tanks, and armor plate. The only thing wrong with the Hien was its engine, which caused constant operational problems through burned out bearings.

By the end of 1944, as a result of bombing of their manufacturing facilities, the Japanese were unable to complete engines rapidly enough to keep up with Ki.61 airframe production. As a result, the Army Air Force insisted that Mitsubishi radial engines be installed in the existing airplanes. This caused considerable engineering trouble, but it resulted in the very finest fighter the Japanese were able to put into the air during the war.

The resultant airplane, which was called Ki.100, was not only superior to the Grumman F6F Hellcat but was at least equal to the North American P-51D Mustang. During one battle a squadron of Ki.100's shot down 14 Hellcats without a single loss to themselves. Fortunately for the Allies, the Ki.100 did not get into full-scale production. Kawasaki completed 2,753 Ki.61's, while only 390 Ki.100's had been delivered by the time the Japanese were forced to surrender.

Other data (Ki.61-KAIC): Wing span, 39 feet 4 inches; length, 29 feet 4 inches; loaded weight, 7,650 pounds; engine, 1,175-horsepower Kawasaki Ha.40; maximum speed, 348 miles per hour at 16,400 feet.

An abandoned Hien on a former Japanese airfield. The plane was one of Japan's finest single-seat fighters.

MITSUBISHI KI.67 HIRYU

Although the Mitsubishi Ki.67 Hiryu (Flying Dragon) first entered combat with the Japanese Navy in October, 1944, as a torpedo-bomber, the plane had actually been designed as a high-level bomber for the Army Air Force. This fact, discovered shortly after by the Allies, caused considerable concern. Until that time Japanese Army bombers had been vulnerable to fighter attack; this new airplane seemed to indicate an end to such vulnerability.

The Imperial Army Air Force leaders realized as early as 1941 that their standard bombers were lacking in several respects and were thus unable to perform the tasks assigned to them with complete effectiveness. The planes then in service did not carry sufficiently large loads of bombs, were too slow, did not have enough protective firepower or armor, and were unable to fly far enough. This realization led to a request to the aircraft industry to develop a fast, modern bomber in the shortest time possible.

When war started in the Pacific, the Japanese were accused of having copied most of their aircraft designs from other nations; some observers also claimed that Japanese workmanship in building their planes was inferior. Neither of these claims was true. In fact, the U.S. Navy admitted in 1945 that Japanese engineering and construction were at least equal to American standards. However, as a result of studies of captured American and British aircraft, some of the features of these were adapted for use in the Ki.67 Hiryu when engineering was started late in 1941.

The original Army specifications called for a bomber with a speed of 310 miles per hour, a radius of action of 620 miles with a bomb load of 1,100 pounds, and an operational altitude of up to 23,000 feet. The Mitsubishi design team decided to try to better all of these demands. When the first experimental model was completed in December, 1942, they found that they had succeeded.

The Army Air Force was enthusiastic over the plane and made plans to put it into immediate mass production. But as Mitsubishi began to tool up, the military started asking for change after change. These alterations resulted in improvements, but they also delayed the program so seriously that only 21 Ki.67's had been completed by April, 1944. However, the Army then gave its approval to standardize production.

When the Ki.67 went into combat, the Army finally had a bomber that was not only fast and with other excellent performance characteristics, but also one that had enough defensive firepower to make it dangerous to attack. By that time, though, production facilities at the manufacturing plants had been badly damaged by an earthquake as well as Allied bombing attacks. Total production of the Ki.67, as result, was only about 700.

Even though the Ki.67 was designed for the Japanese Army, it first went into combat with the Navy as a torpedo-bomber. The plane could do 339 m.p.h. and had good defensive firepower and protective armor.

In addition to its role as a bomber, the Ki.67 was produced in small numbers as a fighter to intercept Boeing B-29 Superfortresses. Normal armament as a bomber was four 12.7-millimeter machine guns and one 20-millimeter cannon. The Ki.109 fighter version had a 75-millimeter cannon plus one 12.7-millimeter gun. Twenty-two Ki.109's were built.

Other data (Ki.67-1B): Wing span, 73 feet 10 inches; length, 61 feet 4 inches; loaded weight, 30,220 pounds; engines, two 1,970-horsepower Mitsubishi Ha.104's; maximum speed, 339 miles per hour at 20,000 feet.

MESSERSCHMITT ME.262 SCHWALBE

The story of the Me.262 is one of unbelievable mixup. All experts agreed, after the war, that if the plane had been produced as soon as it was ready, and as a fighter, the Germans would have achieved complete aerial superiority.

Development work on the Schwalbe (Swallow), which became the world's first jet fighter, was started in 1938. The mock-up was completed in December, 1939, and four months later the German Air Ministry ordered three machines for test purposes.

Because of various delays, the plane was not flown for the first time on pure jet power until July 18, 1942. At that time, however, the Germans thought they could win the war with conventional aircraft and did not see the necessity of building jet fighters in quantity. An order was given to produce only 20 of the machines per month.

When the first planes came from the factory in November, 1943, General Adolf Galland, Commander of the German Fighter Arm, wanted to rush production of the jet as a fighter. But Adolf Hitler interfered, insisting that it be built as a bomber. This brought production to a halt while changes were made, and the Me.262 Sturmvogel (Stormbird) bomber was not flown for the first time until May, 1944.

The bomber version was a failure. When Hitler realized he had been wrong, he ordered the plane

An Me.262 with radar and camouflage for night fighting. These planes might have won the air war for Germany.

The Me.262 was the world's first operational jet fighter. It was considerably faster than any Allied plane.

built as a fighter. But time was running out for the Germans, and the production plan of 1,000 planes per month was never met.

Only 1,294 Me.262's actually left the production lines, most of which never saw combat because of lack of fuel. Those that were flown scored heavily. On one occasion six Schwalbes attacked a formation of 48 B-17 Flying Fortresses and shot down 14 of them. In another battle the Me.262's shot down 25 bombers and five fighters.

As the first operational jet fighter, the Me.262 could have become the most potent weapon in the skies. Because of official delays and interference, the machine had to be written off as one of Germany's worst aviation mistakes.

Other data (Me.262A-1): Wing span, 40 feet 11 inches; length, 34 feet 9 inches; loaded weight, 14,101 pounds; engines, two 1,980-pounds-thrust Junkers Jumo turbojets; maximum speed, 540 miles per hour at 19,684 feet.

No operational fighter with the Allies could have caught the Ar.234, which was the first jet bomber.

ARADO AR.234 BLITZ

In the final stages of World War II the German Air Force was in complete collapse. At the same time, however, its aircraft plants had the finest, most advanced airplanes in the world on their assembly lines. Many of these were jet-propelled, and they had been tested and proved. The Allies lagged so far behind technologically that they were still cautiously testing their first jets.

The Arado Ar.234 Blitz (Lightning) earned its place in aeronautical history as the world's first jet bomber. The plane was so far ahead of its time that the U.S. Air Force did not have a bomber capable of matching its speed until two years after the war had ended, and then only in experimental form. When the Arado first went into operation, the Allies did not have even a piston-engined fighter that could come close to it in performance. One version was actually some 100 miles per hour faster than the fastest Allied single-seater.

The Blitz was projected late in 1940 as the result of a German Air Ministry request for a jet bomber. The specifications called for a maximum speed of not less than 435 miles per hour and a cruising range of not less than 1,242 miles. A design team under Walter Blume, chief engineer of the Arado company, immediately began their studies, and construction of the first test models was started early in 1941. However, development of the Junkers Jumo turbojet engine was going slowly. The first model of the engine had been bench-tested in December, 1940, but the Junkers engineers were not satisfied with its reliability.

The Junkers turbojets were not delivered to the Arado factory until March, 1943. Three months later—June 15—an Ar.234 was finally taken up for its first test flight. One of the experimental models, without military equipment, reached a speed of 557 miles per hour. Two others were fitted with four jet engines. The first of these, the Ar.234V8, was taken up for initial trials on February 1, 1944.

Arado Ar.234's were first flown in the combat area in the fall of 1944. These were unarmed and were used for reconnaissance, flying at altitudes of up to 39,000 feet, where no Allied planes could intercept them. Meanwhile, production had started on the bomber version, which carried an explosive load of 3,300 pounds.

The Germans had planned to build the Ar.234 in volume, but only 150 of the machines were delivered in 1944 and another 64 in 1945. The slow development and production of the plane was a stroke of good fortune for the Allies.

Other data (Ar.234B-2): Wing span, 46 feet 3 inches; length, 41 feet 6 inches; loaded weight, 20,613 pounds; engines, two 1,980-pound-thrust Junkers Jumo turbojets; maximum speed, 461 miles per hour at 19,685 feet.

Above: **This experimental model had four jet engines and reached a speed of 557 m.p.h.** *Below:* **The bomber version carried an explosive load of 3,300 pounds.**

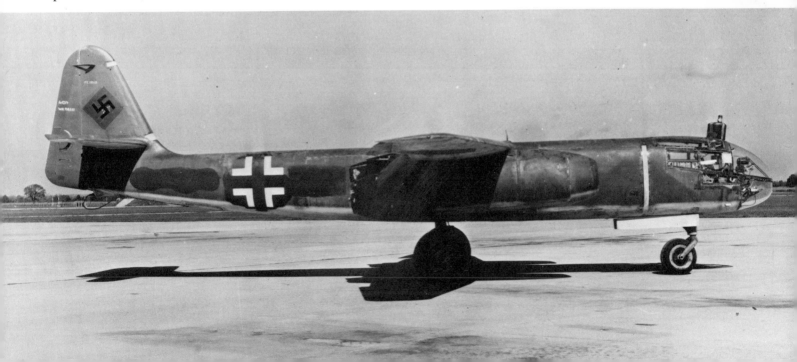

This Shiden-Kai was captured in Japan. It had far heavier armament than any other Japanese fighter.

This is the first N1K seen on the ground by Americans. The airplane was sent to the U.S. for tests.

KAWANISHI N1K SHIDEN

A British aviation expert, following World War II, called the Kawanishi Shiden (Violent Lightning) "the best all-round fighter operational in the Pacific during the entire course of the war." This comment was not made without good reason. The plane met the best the United States and England had to offer, and it proved itself better than most and at least equal to the others.

The plane had a strange history. In August, 1942, Kawanishi completed its first N1K1 Kyofu (Mighty Wind) for the Imperial Navy. The plane was a marine-based fighter, with one large float and two wingtip floats. Despite these floats, it had a top speed of 302 miles per hour and was exceptionally maneuverable.

The military then decided that they also wanted the machine as a land-based fighter. This request caused the Kawanishi design staff considerable difficulty, since they knew they would have to use a very long landing gear so that a large propeller could be installed to realize maximum performance from the 1,990-horsepower engine. The first models of the N1K1-J Shiden were finally made ready for testing before the end of July, 1943.

The first models revealed that the plane had outstanding performance, and it was ordered into production well before the test program was completed. Service models reached the combat area in October, 1944, and war experience soon made its pilots consider the U.S. Navy's Grumman F6F Hellcat a relatively easy victim.

While N1K1-J's were in production, Kawanishi

improved the machine. The new version was designated N1K2-J Shiden-Kai, and it was even better than its predecessor. In one combat a Japanese pilot named Kinsuke Muto used his Shiden-Kai to shoot down four Grumman F6F's out of a formation of 12.

The Navy selected the Shiden-Kai as its major new fighter, and it was ordered into mass production by eight aircraft companies, including Kawanishi. However, this visualized production was made impossible by devastating Boeing B-29 Superfortress raids which virtually destroyed the Japanese aircraft industry. Total production of all versions amounted to only 1,445, including some 425 N1K2-J's.

The Shiden-Kai had the heaviest armament of any Japanese fighter—four 20-millimeter cannon in the wings. One model that did not get into production had two 13.2-millimeter machine guns in addition to the cannon.

Other data (N1J2-J): Wing span, 39 feet 4 inches; length, 30 feet 8 inches; loaded weight, 9,039 pounds; engine, 1,990-horsepower Nakajima Homare (Honor); maximum speed, 369 miles per hour at 18,370 feet.

A Shiden-Kai with American markings. All U.S. pilots who flew the machine reported that it was excellent.

OTHER HISTORIC AXIS PLANES

Above: Italy's Reggiane Re.2001 was first-line in most respects; only 252 were built. *Below:* The German Heinkel He.162 jet had a top speed of 522 m.p.h.

Above: The unorthodox Dornier Do.335 had two engines—one in front, one in the tail. *Below:* Nakajima's B6N was Japan's principal torpedo-bomber in 1944.